The Painted Churches of Romania

JOHN FLETCHER

The Painted Churches of Romania

A Visitor's Impressions

Foreword by ISABEL WYATT

With 42 plates in colour and 8 diagrams

NEW KNOWLEDGE BOOKS 28 Dean Road, London, N.W.2

Printed and bound in Great Britain by R. J. Acford Limited, Industrial Estate, Chichester, Sussex

Contents

List of diagrams in the text

List of illustrations

Acknowledgements

To Isabel Wyatt for her valuable information and correction of the text.

To R. L. Wilson for his advice and help in connection with the text and some of the illustrations and diagrams.

I am indebted to the following books for information concerning the saints mentioned in the text—

'Saints in Folklore' by Christina Hole (G. Bell and Sons).

'Every Man's Book of Saints' by C. P. S. Clarke (A. R. Mowbray & Co.).

'Penguin Dictionary of Saints' by D. Attwater (Penguin).

'The Saints' by John Coulson (Burns and Oates).

'The English Festivals' by Laurence Whistler.

And for information concerning the Eastern Orthodox Church—

'The Eastern Orthodox Church' by R. M. French (Hutchinson University Library).

Pronunciation

Accents

        ţ becomes tza

        ş becomes sh

Voroneţ	=	Vorone*tz*
Moldoviţa	=	Moldovi*tz*a
Suceviţa	=	Sucevi*tz*a
Petru Rareş	=	Rare*sh*
Maramureş	=	Maramure*sh*

Plate I

Plate 2

ROMANIA

U. S. S. R.

HUNGARY

MOLDAVIA

U. S. S. R.

SUCEAVA

CLUJ

BRASOV

GALATI

DANUBE
DELTA

YUGOSLAVIA

BUCHAREST

CONSTANTA

R. DANUBE

BULGARIA

BLACK
SEA

N
W — E
S

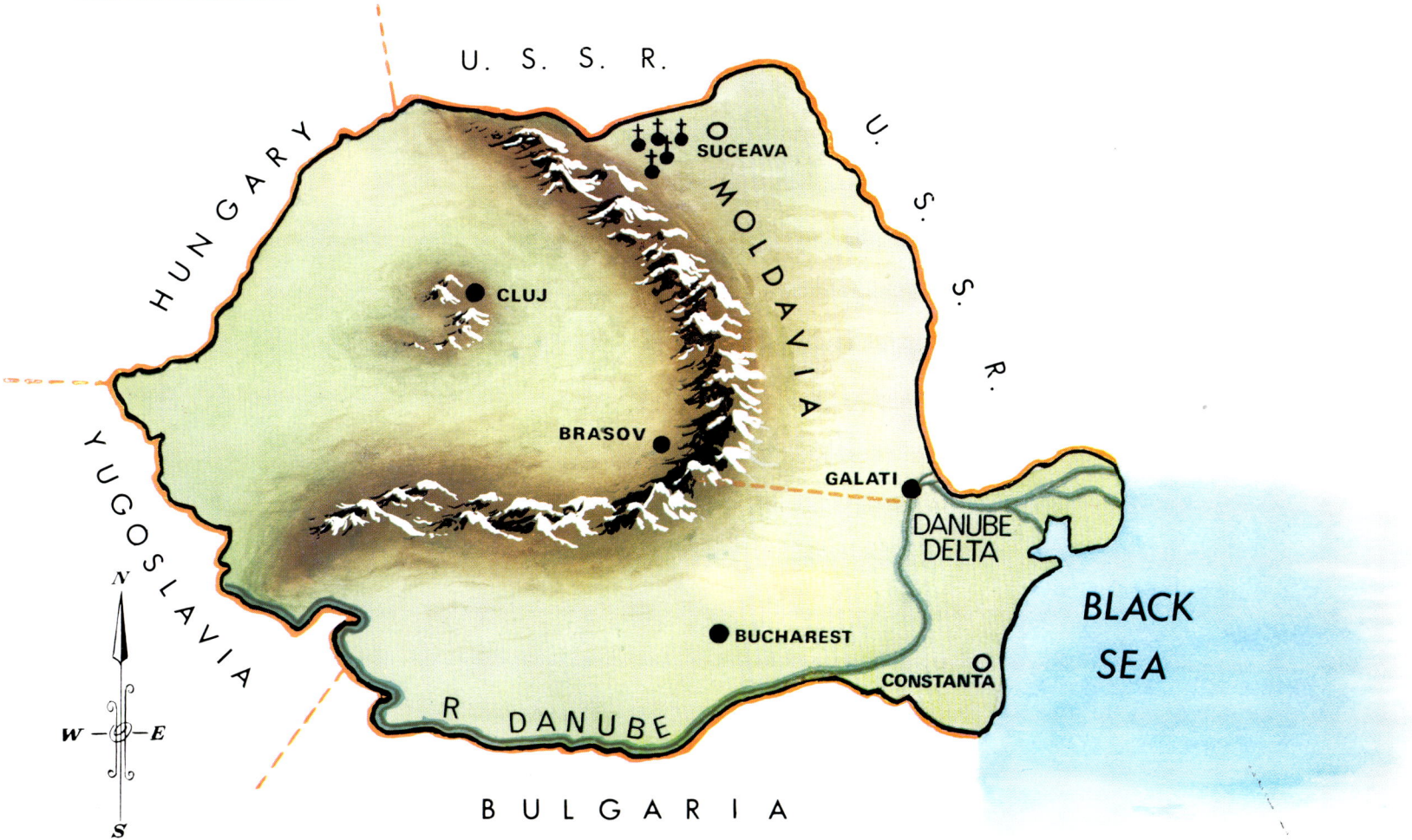

✝ The Five Painted Churches

Foreword

IN THIS NEW BOOK John Fletcher tells the story of his recent pilgrimage to the Painted Churches of Romania, illustrating it with vivid records, from his camera and his brush, of the art-treasures he found there.

What he found there was, in his own words, 'a rejuvenation of Byzantine painting out of its rather rigid application into an inventive, dynamic representation of religious themes in which native artists felt free to introduce folk-lore influences'.

Looking back, we have to remember from what lofty fountain-head Byzantine art originally flowed—it was that high Initiate, Manes, who introduced iconographic painting (as well as choral chanting) into the Early Eastern Church. What later calcified into rigidity came to birth as an attempt to portray the etheric human form. Hence the lack of naturalistic detail, of purely human personality, of background detail, of special depth; it is another dimension than that of the physical that is being presented, and one's response, as one stands face to face and eye to eye with those flat, frontal figures, majestic, archetypal, hieratic, of more than human spiritual stature, takes place at a correspondingly deeper and more inward level. One can well understand how, in less clay-cloistered days, to contemplate such art could have been a powerful pathway into other worlds.

The book's descriptions of the serried ranks of angels at Voroneţ, and of those gathered along the Ladder of Sin at Suceviţa, make one wistfully aware of a former firm sense of commerce with the nearer hierarchies of which we are now bereft. We are reminded of St. John Chrysostom's reference to an esoteric aspect of the celebration of the Mass—' angels surround the priest, with the entire host of celestial powers, filling all the space about the altar'. Because our eyes no longer see them, we have become all too little conscious of the heavenly helpers still walking beside us; such frescoes as these are therefore timely and courage-renewing reminders that higher worlds still inter-penetrate our own.

Such a painting as the one of John the Baptist at Suceviţa, Plate 41, startles us into certainty that either the anonymous artist had deep esoteric knowledge or else that he painted out of a deep esoteric tradition, even if he no longer altogether understood it. St. John carried his own head on a platter; this is something much more than a conventional attribute by which a saint can be identified. It points to a significant secret which Rudolf Steiner has revealed to us.* For Herodias demanded the Baptist's head on a dish for use in degenerate black magic Mysteries; but what she actually did in bringing about his beheading was to free his

---

* Rudolf Steiner: ' *The Last Address* ' Dornach, Sept. 1924 (with a preface by Alfred Heidenreich) Rudolf Steiner Press.

being, first to overshadow and strengthen the Twelve around Christ, and then to unite its own greatness with that of St. John the Divine.

As here, John the Baptist is often portrayed with wings in Byzantine art; it would seem to indicate esoteric knowledge that a very special being was incarnated in him. Rudolf Steiner tells us that John was a reincarnation of the fallen part of Adam and was also overshadowed by Elijah, the great Folk-Spirit of the Jewish people.* It is remarkable that this overshadowing is indicated quite openly in the Gospels. In St. Luke the angel announcing John's coming birth to Zacharias says: ' And he shall go before him in the spirit and power of Elias '. And Christ says in St. Matthew: ' And if ye will believe it, this is Elias, which was for to come '.

But it is only in the light of reincarnation that these sayings become clear; that such knowledge of reincarnation must become increasingly general, Rudolf Steiner intimates in five lectures, *Reincarnation and Karma*. (*Their Significance in Modern Culture.*)†

Perhaps the devils who at Voroneţ bear scrolls on their backs recording the sins committed by the souls being weighed on the scales, and those at Suceviţa who carry in white parcels the sins of the souls on the ladder, may be regarded as among the ' folk-lore influences '. But in the days of picture-thinking this particular ' folk-lore ' was so widespread, in Western as well as in Eastern Christianity, that one feels this ' imagination ' must have a close correspondence to esoteric realities. Thus, Tutivillus, the devil who collected words mumbled in the Mass, appears in the fifteenth century Wakefield Plays, and a bench-end carving at Charlton Mackrell in Somerset depicts him with his bag for these slung over his left shoulder while he himself is recording them on a scroll. When we recall Rudolf Steiner's warning that an unfinished meditation becomes the prey of Ahriman,‡ these Romanian frescoes and this mediaeval ' imagination ' take on a certain cogency.

In his descriptions of what he found on and in the Painted Churches, the writer's joy and wonder, expressed with the soberest sincerity and remarkable translucency, communicate themselves to us, so that we become as active participants in his soul-voyage of discovery as we are in those of Brandon to the Isles of the Blessed or of Mael Duin to the Bridge of Glass.

This adventure, and this book about it, all came out of a walk down Jermyn Street, London. Rarely can a walk down Jermyn Street have been so spiritually rewarding!

ISABEL WYATT

---

* Rudolf Steiner. *The Gospel of St. Luke.* Lecture VI (Basel. Sept. 15–24th 1909). (Rudolf Steiner Press.)
† Rudolf Steiner. *Reincarnation and Karma.* (Rudolf Steiner Press.)
‡ Ahriman (Satan).

Introduction

Before i left England I had read a book called *Europe. A Cosmic Picture,** a posthumous new book by Maria Schindler.

It deals with all the countries of Europe from a very unusual point of view, as Gladys Mayer says in her Introduction—' It is a point of view which links the mysterious movements and order of the Universe of the Stars with the progress of mankind upon the earth . . . Rudolf Steiner at the beginning of this century introduced a new Cosmological and Spiritual Science of man and the Universe. In the sphere of cosmology, Willi Sucher was one of his brilliant pupils '. Maria Schindler was a pupil of Willi Sucher in connection with this cosmology.

As belief in spiritual knowledge decreased, so the science of astrology became decadent and assumed the form found in newspaper horoscopes and other forms of fortune-telling. It was not always so. In Egypt and Babylon it was a great science and by its aid the Pyramids were built; the Druids used it and from it Avebury and Stonehenge arose.

Today it must be brought into line with modern science and become Spiritual Science.

Towards the end of her Introduction Gladys Mayer says—' From her long-developed background of this form of star-wisdom, Maria Schindler has woven a pictorial tapestry of her view of Europe's life-history in all its cosmic earthly and human content '.

In my travels in Russia and many other countries, I have found the contents of this book most illuminating for each of the countries I visited.

So it was to the chapter on the Balkans that I turned before I visited Romania. I can of course only indicate very briefly what she says, sufficient, I hope, to stimulate the reader to read this book himself. As we now live in the age of the ' package ' tour, and are all travellers or potential travellers, we should always be aware of the deeper forces that lie behind the more superficial physical aspects of a given country. The signs of the Zodiac play a very important part in the origin and destiny of the various countries of Europe. Each country is influenced by one of the signs of the Zodiac, for instance, Great Britain by the sign of the Scorpion.

The Balkans, which include Greece and Romania, come under the sign of the Ram, who is the leader of the Zodiac; the other signs of the Zodiac follow him. All the Balkan countries— Greece, Bulgaria, Yugoslavia, Turkey, Albania and Romania—through the Ram forces are connected with the sense of speech. In all the Balkan countries there was and is a distinct tendency towards the appreciation of language. In Romania as well as in Greece the revival of the language was the basic force which led to the creation of the independence of the nation.

Apart from Turkey, their strong religious link is the Eastern Orthodox Church, whose ritual is oriented towards the ' Word '.

---

* *Europe: A Cosmic Picture*. Michael Press, London. (1972)

In the Church of Rome the ritual of the Sacrament is performed in full sight of the congregation but the ' word ' remained alien to the people, for it was spoken in Latin. In the Orthodox Church the ritual of the Sacrament is performed behind the iconastas screen, out of sight of the congregation. The congregation had complete devotion to all that was spoken, to the transmission of the reality of the Sacrament. Worshippers would stand for hours in surrender to the content of their own language, strengthening their souls through the Holy Word.

The Romanian language has its origins in Latin, through the Roman occupation of Dacia, which later became Romania. (This accounts for its similarity to Italian.) It was followed by a Slav influence, which can still be found in the formation of words and syntax. There were also Hungarian, Turkish and Greek influences.

In the eighteenth century Romanian historians discovered Roman connections in their language. Language became the object of much attention. Grammarians were sought out, the most outstanding of whom was Thimotheus Cipariu, whose work contributed greatly to Romania's eventual freedom as an independent nation. During the Hungarian revolution in 1848, he published a manifesto demanding Romania's complete independence. As a result of this manifesto, a great Romanian gathering of 40,000 people assembled in the market square of Blassendorf, which became known as the ' Field of Liberty '. Afterwards they marched through the town in a torchlight procession, the Romanian flag flying, to Cipariu's cottage, where everybody joined in the National Anthem. ' Cipariu opened his window, and replied quite calmly, as if it were not he personally who was being honoured, but the Romanian folk-spirit to which he had devoted his whole life.' Every year on the same date this meeting and procession were repeated.

Cipariu could speak fifteen languages, which he had learned to further the development of the individuality of his people. He died in 1878.

In 1859 Moldavia and Wallachia became united under one Prince, and after the Russo-Turkish War of 1877–78 the Great Powers recognised Romania's independence.

The interest of the Romanians in their language continues to the present day, with the Institute of Linguistics of the Romanian Academy in Bucharest, where they study its history and development. The Academy publishes the periodicals *Linguistic Studies and Research* and *The Romanian Language*. Recently the spelling of Rumania has been changed to Romania, emphasising its Roman origin.

NOTE

"Under the Zodiacal sign of the Ram Romania came to nationhood. The ram points with his head to the future. He demands a new spirituality. As the heavenly Ram turns his gaze into the future, so the nations of south-eastern Europe will look towards the aquisition of faculties that contain the seed of future development.

The Archangel who guides these peoples looks into the future. Nothing he has achieved so far was repetition; everything was transformation. Into his distant goal he incorporated the impulses of the word, and on the path to the future he succeeded in awakening his people. But their development towards the formation of states is again only the first premonition of different future possibilities, whose attainment will require a long period of hard striving.

What was preserved as a selfless and devoted Christianity in south-eastern Europe throughout centuries of complete isolation will arise in the individual human being of that future with a strength as yet beyond our imagination.

Then the Word will no longer work as a power confined to a certain nation. Peoples merely prepare the path. The spoken word, strengthened through all it has transmitted in the course of time from man to man, will one day, as healer and awakener, transform evil through love." (Extract from Maria Schindler's *Europe: A Cosmic Picture*, for further details read Rudolf Steiner's lectures.)*

* Rudolf Steiner: ' Anthroposophical ' Life Gifts Lecture Cycle 49, Berlin, 1918.
* Rudolf Steiner: ' How Anthroposophical Groups Prepare for the Sixth Epoch', Dusseldorf, June 1915.

14

Bucharest

THE PAINTED CHURCHES of Romania or rather Moldavia are unique in Europe. Individual painted churches can be found in Spain and Russia, but nowhere else can there be found a group of churches, comparatively close together, with all the exterior walls painted with murals, as in Romania.

They are situated in a very remote part of the country, in the far north near the Russian frontier, in the Carpathian mountains.

They are nearly unknown in England and it was by chance I heard about them.

I was walking down Jermyn Street in London one day during the winter and passing the Romanian Travel Office when in the window I saw a large coloured photograph of the most amazing church I had ever seen. It was glowing with colour underneath its great curving roof, the exterior walls being covered with murals from ground level to roof. I went inside, to be told that there were five such churches covered with exterior paintings in a small area in northern Moldavia, a province of Romania.

So one day during the summer found me in the Orient Express bound for Bucharest, well behind the Iron Curtain.

The journey through lush, opulent Germany and Austria from Munich, Salzburg on to Vienna, was in striking contrast, after passing the frontier into Hungary, to the sparseness and utility behind the Iron Curtain. It was perhaps fitting that I should arrive in Budapest in the middle of a terrific thunderstorm, with a profusion of lightning and the roar of the thunder like a volcano and a hurricane-like wind sweeping down upon the city; these elemental forces seemed still to be echoing the forces raised by the Hungarian revolt in 1956.

It was interesting to travel across the vast Hungarian plains before reaching the Romanian frontier at midnight. During the night the train passed through the province of Transylvania, legendary home of Dracula and vampires—the setting for the Dracula stories.

Early the next morning we were passing through the Carpathian mountains, which in places rise to 8,000 ft. These mountains, coming from the north in a semi-circle, isolate Transylvania from the rest of the country.

Out of the mountains the train came down into the great Romanian plain which stretches to the Black Sea, and at noon we arrived in Bucharest (Bucuresti), the capital.

The spaciousness of the station, the Gara de Nord, very clean and bright with flowers, is reflected in the broad tree-lined streets of the city. My hotel, unpretentious but comfortable, was next door to an old white Byzantine church. My terms were inclusive, with everything paid before I left England. In Russia I had paid for my meals with meal coupons given me each day by the Tourist Bureau, but in Romania I was given meal money every day.

Compared with Russia, the shops are well stocked, but in both countries the best-stocked shops and the most crowded are the bookshops. The Romanians are very lively and in their character and language very like the Italians. I read a story in a magazine about a Romanian who had spent his holiday in Italy and when he returned he was asked how he had enjoyed himself; he said very much, but they spoke Romanian with a terrible accent. For the Romanian, conversation and the animated café life are his two chief entertainments.

Bucharest had once been capital of Wallachia only, but in 1862, a few years after the union of Moldavia and Wallachia, it became capital of the new nation—Romania. In the following years industry and business flourished and the city became known as ' the Paris of the Balkans '.

In the centre of the city is the former Royal Palace, now the Palace of the People's Republic, residence of the President of the Republic. In a wing of this palace is the National Art Gallery where there is a fine *Adoration of the Shepherds* by El Greco and a comprehensive collection of icons. The palace is guarded by soldiers, their uniform rather similar to that of the Russians. The changing of the guard is quite interesting; the guards march in slow time with a sort of ' goose step '. Near the palace, but dwarfed by blocks of modern flats, is a beautiful Byzantine church of red brick. This is called the Cretulescu Church (1722) (Plates 3, 4), the two towers with their domes being unusually tall for a Byzantine church. There are fine frescoes in the interior and in the porch. This church and others in Bucharest show how the Byzantine style was transformed into its own national style, a sort of Romanian style, similar to the way in which the Byzantine in Russia became Russianised. These churches in Bucharest are mostly eighteenth century, some 200 years later than the Painted Churches we shall be seeing in Moldavia. Hidden away in a side street is the beautifully proportioned Stavropoleas Church, (1824), with an exterior very colourful with murals.

In the outskirts of Bucharest, in a setting of woods, lakes and gardens, is the Village Museum (Muzeul Satului), consisting of stone and wooden houses with thatched or shingled roofs, completely furnished even to the icons on the walls. There are over 300 different structures, including windmills, brought from every district of Romania. Among them are three very interesting and unusual wooden churches, two from the Maramureş district of the province of Transylvania.

In Transylvania there are still a thousand of these wooden churches (sixteenth to eighteenth centuries). Those in the Maramureş are the finest and of these, those on a road from Sighet which goes along the Iza Valley are the best (Plate 7). Some of these have no iron or stone in their construction, and one small church was hewn out of the solid trunk of an oak tree.

Their chief characteristics are a low spreading shingled roof almost reaching the ground, and a beautiful slender tower rising out of the high double-spreading roof, with a spire becoming ever more slender, like a finger pointing to heaven; on the top is an elaborate cross. The sanctuary has its own conical shaped roof. The church with the highest spire, 180 feet high, is at Surdesti. These churches also have beautifully carved porches, windows and gateways.

The two examples in the Village Museum are very characteristic. The largest, which stands on a bank above a lake, dominating the whole village with its soaring slender spire (from the village of Dragomiresti in Maramureş) is dated 1722.

The other church from the village of Turea near Cluj is dated 1750. Though small it is strange and fascinating, standing in a glade surrounded by trees; at a distance it seems all

Communism claims to be regarded as a religion in itself, inasmuch as it has its own philosophy of life which is totalitarian in character and seeks to control every aspect of life. The crux of the conflict lies in the fact that Christianity also claims the whole man, body, soul and spirit, and neither can, in theory, tolerate the existence of another total allegiance. The clash is emphasized by the fact that Communism regards this other allegiance as an aberration of the human mind, and the idea of the spiritual principle in man as an illusion. I am indebted to the book *The Eastern Orthodox Church* by the Rev. R. M. French for the above information.*

All visitors to Communist countries behind the Iron Curtain should read for a deeper understanding of the ideology of Karl Marx *The Tension between East and West* by Rudolf Steiner, a cycle of ten lectures given in Vienna in 1922. It is remarkable that only four years after the Russian Revolution, Rudolf Steiner was able to write: ' The spectre of Eastern Europe gazes threateningly across to the West. Its gaze, however, should not leave us inactive, but should be a challenge to us to seek at every moment for vital social forces and vital formulation of social needs, now that the abstract and Utopian ones have revealed their unfruitfulness.'

In the lectures that follow in the book he describes how this can be achieved.†

---

* *The Eastern Orthodox Church.* R. M. French. (Hutchinson's University Library.)
† Rudolf Steiner. *The Tension Between East and West.* (Hodder and Stoughton.)

Bucharest

Plate 3
Cretulescu Church.
(1722) north-east
Bucharest.
Built in the Wallachian
style, which was developed
during the reign of Prince
Constantin Brincoveanu
(1688-1714). The two
cupolas are unusually tall.

Plate 4
Cretulescu Church
north-west. There are
murals in the porch and in
the interior.

Plate 6
Wooden church from
Rapciuni, district of
Ceahlau (1773). *Village
Museum*, Bucharest. The
belfry is above the porch,
which has a wealth of
wood-carving.

History of Romania : A short table of dates

A.D. 105	Roman province.
275	Occupied by the Goths.
400–1400	Occupied by the Huns, the Bulgars and Slavs.
1300	Wallachia and Moldavia founded.
1457–1504	Stephen the Great, Prince of Moldavia.
1504–1547	Prince Petru Rareş. (The son of Stephen the Great.)
1538	Moldavia occupied by the Turks.
1530–1604	The Painted Churches completed.
1593–1601	Michael the Brave. Prince of the united states of Wallachia, Moldavia and Transylvania.
1859	Wallachia and Moldavia united to become Romania.
1877–1878	Turks driven out.
1881	Prince Charles of Hohenzollern crowned Carol 1st.
1940	Carol abdicated and his son Michael crowned King.
1940	Occupied by the Germans.
1944	Liberated by the Russians.
1944	A coalition government formed of left and centre parties.
1947	King Michael abdicated and a republic proclaimed. The Communists rapidly gained control.
	The Russian Army, which had expelled the Germans in 1944, remained in Romania until 1958.

Suceava (Moldavia)

MOLDAVIA'S GOLDEN AGE, outstanding in the whole of Europe, flourished during the reigns of Stephen the Great, the warrior Prince of Moldavia who became an almost legendary hero in his fight against the Turks, and of his son Petru Rareş.

During this period, churches, palaces, monasteries, all enclosed by fortified walls and watch towers, were erected all over Moldavia. It was behind these ramparts that this 'golden age' arose, despite the constant threat of the formidable Turk, and even continued after the Turks had invaded the country and defeated Petru Rareş in 1538.

Stephen the Great, through his great personal magnetism and the inspiration of the Romanian folk-spirit, inaugurated this 'golden age'. It reached its climax, during the reign of Petru Rareş, in the creation of fourteen churches with marvellous painted exteriors.

Of these fourteen original Painted Churches five have survived with their exterior paintings more or less intact after 400 years of wars, occupation by the Turks, and severe winters.

It seems almost a miracle that the Turks did not destroy these Painted Churches, which to them must have appeared as citadels of spiritual resistance.

A significant point to remember is that these Byzantine churches came into being over fifty years after the Turks had captured Constantinople, thus cutting off the spiritual stream of Eastern Christianity from its source. This resulted in a rejuvenation of Byzantine painting out of its rather rigid application into an inventive, dynamic representation of religious themes. In these themes native artists felt free to introduce folklore influences and local themes such as the Life of St. John the New and such as sinners represented as Turks.

They are all situated within an approximate radius of sixty miles from Suceava. Four are: *Humor 1535. Arbore 1541. Moldoviţa 1542. Voroneţ 1547.* (The dates refer to the year when the paintings were either commenced or completed.)

The fifth, the *Suceviţa Monastery*, was founded in 1584 and painted in 1601. This was rather strange, as although it had seemed that the extraordinary phenomenon of the Painted Churches had come abruptly to an end many years previously, it suddenly blossomed again at the turn of the century.

For the seventeenth century the folk-spirit had other tasks for the Romanian people; but one can see Suceviţa, the largest of these monasteries and the one with the most complete paintings, as a precious casket to be carried forward into future centuries.

Mention must also be made of another Romanian hero—Michael the Brave, the first prince to unite the three Romanian principalities of Wallachia, Transylvania and Moldavia into a single state. His aim was 'to make out of our poor country a shield for the whole world'

20

against the Turkish invasion. Unfortunately this union was only temporary, and the country had to await the fulfilment of its destiny until 1918, when all three principalities were again united.

The town of Suceava was the ancient capital of Moldavia up to 1565. Stephen the Great and his son Petru Rareş reigned here and lived in the great castle, now ruined, though the moat and drawbridge still survive. There are a number of mediaeval churches; the most imposing is the Church of the Monastery of St. George, with tall towers and a very colourful red-orange glazed tiled roof. It is the burial place of St. John the New, patron saint of Moldavia; here his relics are preserved.

Stephen the Great founded monasteries other than those which had painted churches. At one of these at Putna he himself is buried.

The town on its hill is placed in a beautiful countryside, surrounded by old-world villages of wooden houses and fir-clad hills merging into the foothills of the Carpathian mountains.

I arrived in Suceava late at night in a violent thunderstorm and pouring rain. The car I had ordered was not there; I got the last bus just as it was leaving. The town is two miles from the station. The bus stopped in the bus station and I was left in the pouring rain to find my way to the hotel, but a young man passing who spoke English picked up my case and took me to the hotel. Such kindness I was to experience quite often.

The next day was bright and sunny, and I had the task of organizing a car to take me to the Painted Churches. I discovered the price would be very high; there were no tourist excursions to the churches. (I did this trip to Romania when the travel allowance was only £50.) Then a Romanian lady with an Italian friend offered to share a car with me. It was Midsummer's Day. What better day, for it was to prove a visit to Fairyland.

The Painted Churches

Humor

Plate 13
Humor.
South façade with southern
lateral apse. The
undulating wooden roof is
shingled.

Plate 14
Humor.
South façade from the
corner of the open western
porch to the southern
lateral apse and the eastern
apse.
The paintings on the left
half wall centred on the
Gothic window represent
the Invocation Hymn to
the Holy Virgin with the
Invocation to St. Nicholas
and the Prodigal Son on the
right half.

Plate 16
Humor.
The paintings on the south
lateral and eastern apses
depict the Procession of
Saints, which consists of
saints, apostles and
martyrs, moving in
hierarchical order towards
the east.

Humor

As WE SET out towards the mountains and the Painted Churches, we found the roads crowded with horse-carts loaded with men and women dressed in their national costume, coming into Suceava to the Midsummer festival at the Church of St. George.

After having passed through numerous villages of wooden houses and many flocks of ducks and geese, we came to the first of the Painted Churches set in a valley surrounded by wooded hills and close to the clear waters of the Humor river. Beyond a large detached wooden belfry, the church stood there in all its glowing colours, in a bower of green lawns. (Plate 8.)

A wide fir-tree shingled roof with fascinating undulating curves protected the treasures below. I was reluctant to leave my rather distant view-point and go closer to examine the details as it was the whole ' ensemble ' that was so fascinating, the perfect harmony of colour and form, with the roof reflecting the curves of the surrounding hills.

I was entirely in agreement with the words of my little guide book—' Nothing like this can be found in another country '.

I moved round to the west-façade, which has an unusual open porch, an architectural feature appearing for the first time, in contrast to the usual closed porch. It was to be repeated only once, at Moldoviţa, and then disappeared for a hundred years to reappear transformed.

Here is a foundation stone written in Old Slavonic—'. . . by the will and the help of the merciful Prince Petru Voirod, son of old Prince Stephen, this church was founded and built at the expense and by the labour of God's serf Boyar Teodor, great captain, and his wife Anastasia, in the year 7038 (1530).' The frescoes were done in 1535.

On all the surfaces of the four pointed arches of the porch, and also on the back walls, are well preserved paintings of scenes of the Last Judgment, one of the main themes of all five Painted Churches. On one of the arches of the porch, the three warrior saints, St. George, St. Demetrius and St. Mercurius are shown riding into battle; these panels are very dynamic.

The paintings on the southern façade are amazingly well preserved, being sheltered from the fierce northerly winter winds from Russia. From the porch to the border pattern near the centre of the wall there is depicted the theme of the Invocation Hymn to the Holy Virgin who, according to a legend, saved the city of Constantinople in A.D. 626 when it was attacked by the Persians. To the right of the Gothic window is a magnificent composition, The Virgin's Council, which stands out from all the other painted panels by virtue of its size and oval shape. In the panels at the bottom showing the Siege of Constantinople (nearly all of which are damaged), the Persians are dressed as Turks. From the central decorative border to the south lateral apse the Invocation to St. Nicholas is depicted. (Plates 13, 14, 15.)

The paintings on the lateral and altar apses are most impressive, the forms and colours being very well preserved; the theme is the Procession of Saints, which include prophets, apostles and martyrs moving in hierarchical order towards the axis of the altar. Christ and Mary are guarded by the Archangel Michael. (Plate 16.)

The paintings on the north façade are in poor condition, due to the severe winter weather. The themes are the Tree of Jesse and St. George's Invocation.

I entered the church through the open porch, by the early sixteenth century Gothic door. Moldavian religious architecture had mastered the inner layout, which consisted of the porch, or narthex, the pronaos, then the nave and the altar. The whole area behind the iconastas (the icon screen) is called the altar.

The internal paintings follow the usual Byazantine iconographic scheme, covering all the walls of the interior. Among them is an interesting panel showing St. Marina holding a devil by his hair with her left hand, and an upraised hammer with her right.

The interior of an Eastern Orthodox church is very different from a Western church (see Fig. 1, page 27), the essential difference being in the iconastas, the great screen, which stretches across the width of the church, completely shutting off the altar from the nave.

Even the name *altar* does not mean the same as it does in the Western Church. In the Eastern Church, the altar is not the name of a thing but of a place, i.e. that part of the church in which the altar—in the Western sense—stands. The Eastern name for the altar is the Throne. Thus in Orthodox parlance the Throne stands in the altar.

The iconastas has three doors, the Royal Doors in the centre and two smaller doors one on either side.

The iconastas is covered with icons, those on, over, or around the Royal Doors being the most important.

The centre of the first tier of icons above the doors is occupied by the Deesis, a triple icon showing the Christ enthroned, with the Virgin Mary on His right and St. John the Baptist on His left, which can be considered the heart of the iconastas. It is flanked on either side by the Archangels Gabriel and Michael and the twelve Apostles, and all the icons on the screen have the faces of the figures turned towards it. The iconastas is the meeting place of heaven and earth.

The main part of the service takes place behind the iconastas with the doors closed, except when the priest may, from time to time, open the doors for prayers, or the side doors for processions. At the climax of the service the Royal Doors are opened and the priest, holding the chalice with bread and wine in it, administers the Sacrament to the congregation, as they come up to the Royal Doors to receive it.

The iconastas divides the nave from the altar (the sanctuary). The nave is flanked on either side, north and south, by semi-circular apses, and the whole of the altar is in the semi-circular eastern apse. From these three semi-circular apses the church extends westward in the form of a rectangle. This geometrical form applies to all the Painted Churches except Arbore, which has only an eastern apse.

The origin of the eastern apse is interesting. Norwich Cathedral, unlike nearly all the other Norman Cathedrals, which were altered to the rectangular during the Gothic period, still retains its eastern apse, and all the cathedrals built in the new style had an earthly rectangular east end, thus losing the cosmic circular form. This was a development unique to England. In Norwich the High Altar still stands in the circular apse, behind which, raised on steps, is the ancient Bishop's throne.

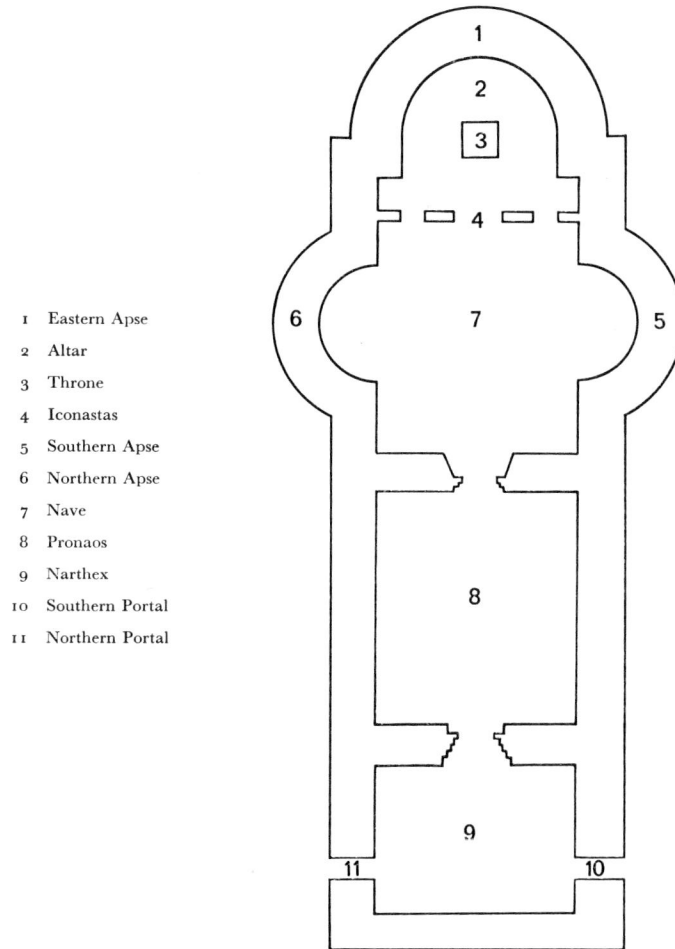

1   Eastern Apse
2   Altar
3   Throne
4   Iconastas
5   Southern Apse
6   Northern Apse
7   Nave
8   Pronaos
9   Narthex
10 Southern Portal
11 Northern Portal

Fig. 1. Simplified ground plan of Voroneṭ.

In the *Pictorial History of Norwich Cathedral* Canon Gilbert Thurlow says that the Norwich Bishop's throne is a unique survival, in England, of the primitive plan, practically universal in Christian cathedrals for several centuries, and that ' the tradition behind the Norwich throne goes back far beyond the eighth century—indeed to the beginning of Christianity itself'. He goes on to say that the earliest Christian worship took place in borrowed buildings, in the pillared halls where the pre-Christian Mysteries had their meetings. The Mystery Hall consisted of a hall with aisles and a semi-circular apse. In the centre of the apse raised on steps, was the throne; on each side were seats.

The Roman Law Court and the Jewish Synagogue had a similar lay-out, so it would be natural for the Early Christian Church to follow the same plan. The circle has a deep spiritual meaning, well-known in those early days.

Going back to pre-historic times, Stonehenge consisted of several concentric circles and, on the Helestone, the midsummer sun, a circle filled with light, appeared at sunrise.

Fig. 2. The Helestone, Stonehenge.

In a Christianized form this appeared again through the wisdom of the Irish–Scottish monks; in the Celtic crosses the cosmic solar circle is within the crosshead. The early Christians knew of Christ's connection with the Sun.

In pre-Christian times it was known that a great spiritual Being was approaching the earth from the spiritual region of the Sun. The Celtic Christians felt strongly that the Christ descended to the earth from the sun-realm; therefore the circle appears round the crosshead representing the radiating Sun of Christ.

In the construction of a Celtic cross, the right angles of the crosshead have to become semi-circles to allow the light to shine through the circle; on some Celtic crosses the circle unites the outside ends of the crosshead. (Figs. 3, 4.)

So the Celtic cross, standing on its square base and in a rectangle moving to the circle at the top, recalls the ground plan of these five Romanian churches. One can feel that the top of the circle in the apse is completed at the bottom in the nave behind the congregation, who stand within the circle, as they receive the Sacrament in front of the Royal Doors.

Fig. 6, on page 29 indicates the simplified ground plan of Arbore, the only one of the five churches with a single apse.

In Christian church-architecture there is a connection between the cosmic circle and the earthly cross or rectangle; as Paul Paede says in his article *Stonehenge and the Cathedral of Coventry*†—'the circle lives on in the apse which is added to the cross-shaped or rectangular ground-plan. The apse is a halved central building (Jansen) containing the heart-piece of the church '.

Fig. 3. Celtic Cross, Monasterboice, Ireland.

Fig. 4. A Celtic Cross.

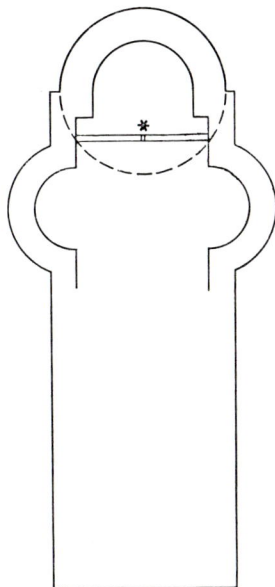

* The Royal Doors, Iconastas.

Fig. 5. Simplified Ground Plan of the Painted Churches.

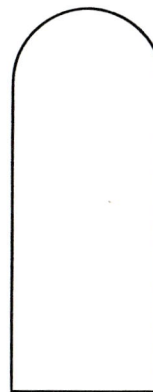

Fig. 6. Ground Plan of Arbore.

In Voroneţ, Moldoviţa and Suceviţa, the cosmic circle is emphasized by three apses, three semi-circles, like the semi-circles on the Celtic crosses Fig. 3 and Fig. 4; the eastern apse protects the sanctuary and the northern and southern apses protect the congregation, who are standing in the rectangular nave facing the iconastas screen.

† Published in the *Anthroposophic News Sheet*. July 1968.

In Sir Banister Fletcher's *A History of Architecture* (On the Comparative Method), it is interesting to compare the ground plan of Christian churches from the Early Christian days to the end of the Gothic period.

The Church of the Nativity, Bethlehem, has a simplified ground plan very similar to the four painted churches, having an eastern apse, a southern and northern apse.

The Church of the Holy Sepulchre, Jerusalem, has the cosmic circle emphasized very strongly; the Sepulchre is situated in the middle of a complete circle, which is situated in the eastern apse. There are no lateral apses; instead the western end of the inner nave is formed into an apse.

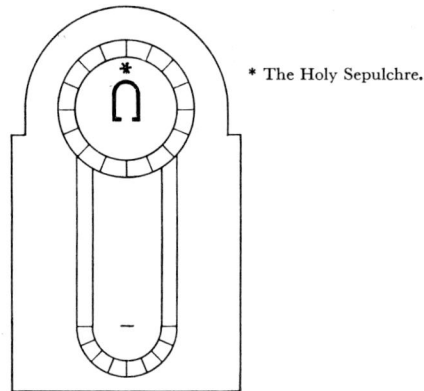

* The Holy Sepulchre.

Fig. 7. Simplified Ground Plan of the centre of the Church of the Holy Sepulchre, Jerusalem.

Apart from Bethlehem I could find only three other churches with the threefold apse like the Romanian churches.

1. At the Church of the Apostles, Cologne (German Romanesque).
2. The Church of St. Elizabeth, Marburg (German Gothic).
3. The Cathedral of S. Maria del Fiori, Florence (Italian Gothic), where the exceptionally long nave opens into three immense apses.

The ground-plan of these four Romanian painted churches is therefore exceptionally rare.

But it is the exterior paintings that have made Humor as well as the other four Painted Churches famous all over Europe. So I passed quickly outside and, once again standing at a distance, gazed at those walls covered with glowing colours underneath that widespread fascinating roof.

The monastery church was surrounded by an enclosing wall with fortified towers; only one of the towers has survived, and none of the walls. As the foundations of the walls can be traced, it is intended to rebuild them.

30

Voroneț

Plate 17
Voronet.
The church from the
south-west. West façade:
The Last Judgement.
South façade: Tree of Jesse.

Plate 18
Voroneţ.
West façade: The Last
Judgement.

Plate 20
Voronet.
Detail of Last Judgement.
The Gates of Paradise.
Lower row, left, St. Peter
holding the keys leads
St. Paul by the hand, to
the right of the same row
are David and Solomon,
wearing crowns.

Plate 21
Voroneţ.
South façade: Detail of the
Tree of Jesse.

Plate 23
Voroneţ.
Interior of the nave.
Stephen the Great presents
a model of the church to
Christ, behind him stands
St. George.

Moldovița

Plate 27
Moldoviṭa.
Eastern apse and the main
gateway.

Voroneţ

Two MILES UP the valley from Humor I came to Voroneţ, nestling under the steep slopes of fir-clad mountains, close to the Voroneţ and Magherniţa rivers. Even immediately following the beauties of Humor, Voroneţ amazed me. The description in my little guide book was so exact—' Looked at from a distance, the building appears like a brightly-illuminated Bible, lying open in a dark green meadow.'* (Plate 9.)

The exterior is very imposing as one looks towards the eastern apse, the great steeple with its circular shingled roof, with the wide spreading, undulating shingled roof underneath, repeating the circular movement of the apse. This is where the Gothic combines harmoniously with the Byzantine and thus produces the characteristic Moldavian style. (Plate 10.)

The walls of the apses underneath glowed with colour. I moved round the building, still keeping at a distance, and looked at it from the south-west. (Plate 17.) The southern wall from the apse to the narthex is a lovely cobalt blue (the blue background of Voroneţ is famous), with the figures appearing in various shades of red, orange and gold, contrasted with white on this blue background. I had hardly recovered from the beauty of this wall when, as I moved slowly westwards, the western façade dawned on my astonished gaze. A most dramatic composition covered the entire west wall, which does not have a porch, so the whole space was available for it. The wall has a slight curve, caused by buttresses coming from the north and south sides, which gives a slight enclosing effect. From this great expanse of surface every colour imaginable shines out, wonderfully harmonious in the westering sunlight. Gold and blue predominate, with contrasting colours of various reds, dark green, white and black.

Above it the vast overspreading undulating shingled roof spreads its protecting wings. This is the famous Last Judgement, the most dramatic and certainly the most arresting exterior Last Judgement in the whole world. (Plates 18, 19, 20.)

It was this church, photographed from this aspect, that I had seen on that dark winter's day in London, brilliant in its colours, in the window of the Romanian Travel Office.

I now moved round to the north façade. Though here the wild winter storms from Russia had played havoc with the quality of the paintings, interesting scenes can still be made out. High up on the wall under the protection of the roof, there is the strange theme called Adam's Writ, a folk-belief not known to the Church. Adam, after being driven out of the Garden of Eden, makes a bargain with Satan to cultivate the land in Satan's possession. Adam in return was to give Satan all the souls of his descendants. The folk-tale relates that Jesus broke the pact.

---

* *Voroneţ* by Petru Comarnescu. Meridiane Publishing House, Bucharest.

I now returned to the Last Judgement to examine it in more detail. My little guide book, which has quite an artistic descriptive text, stresses the importance of this composition being regarded as a whole and looked at from various distances; the great variety of scenes and the manner in which the colours are used in the different scenes only cause confusion unless one stands at the right distance. This of course should apply to all works of art. Alas, so many books on art concentrate on the details and one longs to see the whole setting. This is especially important in viewing all these Painted Churches.

Looking at this great composition we see in the middle of the top panel angels in flight holding open a triptych of a picture of God. This is set in the midst of a parchment scroll held open at each end by a group of four angels, depicting the Signs of the Zodiac; the animals of the Zodiac have fish tails.*

In the centre of the next panel below, the Christ is shown in a circle of radiance, golden rays on a white background, the Christ as the Sun-being. Grouped behind are the divine Hierarchies. On the left and right with bowed heads stand the Virgin Mary and St. John the Baptist. Two groups of apostles are seated on a bench on either side of this central group. Their brightly coloured garments and their individual expressions are remarkable. Behind them are seated rows of angels, their haloes giving a radiant golden background. At Christ's feet there is the source of the Gehenna, the red river of fire that flows, becoming ever broader, on its way down to Hell.

The third panel below represents the Seat of Judgement; from a hand appearing underneath hang the Scales.

On the left St. Paul leads the devout—believers, martyrs and prophets—towards the Judgement Seat. On the right Moses shows the sinners the way down the river of fire to Hell. The sinners are represented as Turks, who defeated Prince Petru Rareș and conquered the country. Great determination and brutality is shown in their very individual expressions, and their turbans are most impressive in their variety.

The left half of the fourth panel is connected with the panel below, that of Paradise. The right half shows the sinners who are being weighed in the scales. A group of angels is gathered round the left hand balance. One of the angels has a long spear with which he is trying to defend the naked sinners against the devils. The devils carry scrolls on their backs, which show the sins committed. On the right hand scale is a bundle of scrolls, with devils sitting on them, trying to bring the scale down; nearby an angel with outspread wings, judging by his size an archangel, attacks a devil with his spear.

Across the river of fire in the right hand corner of the panel is shown the Resurrection of the Dead on the Last Day, which is continued below in the fifth panel. The scene above represents the resurrection of those souls who died on land and the one below those who died at sea. Great imagination is shown in these two scenes. A rather oriental-looking goddess presides over the land, while a Greek-looking goddess, riding a dolphin, presides over the sea. All sorts of animals can be seen in both scenes, swarming round the tombs and on the shore of the sea—lions, bears, wolves, dragons, etc. Each scene has its archangel; instead of a trumpet

_____

* See note The Voroneț Signs of the Zodiac on page 49.

32

they use the lucium, long alpine wooden horns, such as the Romanian shepherds still use in the mountains. Close by, King David plays a Romanian cobza (a lute).

It is these characteristics that make the details so fascinating, the Romanian folk-art breaking the more usual rigid Byzantine style. It is interesting to remember how the Byzantine style was transformed when it was taken to Russia and how the Byzantine style was blended with Norman and Arabian influences in Sicily.

The last panels, lower left of the river of fire, are remarkable. The scenes are set in Paradise and harmoniously combined. Rows of saints are gathered together, waiting to enter the gate of Paradise, although only those in the front row are shown with their whole body; the vast concourse behind them is suggested by the rows of haloes disappearing into the distance. The most interesting group in the Paradise scenes is the centre one leading down from the fourth panel to the fifth panel. To begin with, only haloes can be seen, then foreheads, then a row of heads looking to the right, then a row of heads looking to the left, the diagonal alignment of the heads giving rhythm and movement to this scene. This brings one down to the front row where, on the left nearest the gate, St. Peter holds the keys and leads St. Paul by the hand, while on the right of the same row are David and Solomon, wearing crowns.

Above the southern portal and on either side of the Gothic window are twelve panels which depict the life of St. John the New, patron saint of Moldavia. The scenes show his martyrdom, his assailants being dressed as Turks, and the carrying of his coffin with his relics to the church of St. George in Suceava. On a large panel to the left of the portal is an impressive St. George and the Dragon, showing the princess leading the dragon by her girdle and St. George riding on his white horse.

I moved round to the south façade. Dominating this wall is a vast composition depicting the Tree of Jesse. The whole theme emerges from a lapis lazuli blue background. The Tree of Jesse represents the spiritual and physical ancestors of the earthly vehicle of the Christ. The ' tree ' spreads its branches out over the wall in all directions, the branches intertwine and from the flowers rise these ancestors, the shapes of the flowers being used to produce the figures. They are very decorative, lotus flowers, bluebells, tulips and the bindweed from the local meadows; strangely enough, among these ancestors are ancient Greek philosophers including Plato. The angle of some of the heads looking upward is very unusual. I sent a postcard of a group to a friend, who wrote back saying, ' The Tree of Jesse is the loveliest and most delicate I have ever seen; the two lower figures have a head posture anatomically impossible, yet most convincing in their sense of attention, single-mindedly concentrated on what they (the ancestors of Jesus of Nazareth) see—the vision of the Child to be descended from them'. (Plate 21.)

As the southern façade merges into the eastern apses, quite a different sort of composition is depicted—a great procession of saints winds round the apses to the northern façade. (Plate 22.)

This side of the church is a masterpiece of harmonious blending of the paintings with the architecture.

That these exterior paintings have survived 400 years, of which 200 years were under

Turkish domination, is remarkable. The technique used is that of fresco; water-colours are used on a wet wall, the plaster being made of slaked lime, sand and chopped straw. The famous Voroneț blue came from lapis lazuli. The various colours used were made more waterproof by mixing with cow's bile and egg yolk.

I entered the church by a very beautiful Gothic portal which brings one into the narthex, the rectangular western end of the church, then through another door into the pronoas and the nave which leads to the icon screen and the altar. The walls of the nave, altar and domes are covered with paintings dating from Stephen the Great's reign (1488).

In the nave is a votive painting of Stephen and his family, which shows Stephen the Great, founder of the church, holding in his hands the model of the church, which he offers to Christ, who is seated, dressed in purple. St. George, patron saint of Voroneț, is between Stephen and Christ, slightly to the rear, and his right arm is round Stephen's shoulder. His left hand is raised eloquently, his head is turned towards Christ, and the whole gesture is as if he were presenting Stephen and the church to Christ. Stephen's face is reputed to be a true likeness, and behind him is his wife Maria Voicița, with their daughter and son Alexandru on either side of her. (Plate 23.)

The portraits of the donors who founded churches are common in Byzantine frescoes, reminding the observer of the person who had inspired the building. They were intermediaries between religion and the onlookers, the believers and subjects of the powerful person they represented. As they were painted in company with saintly figures this made the donor's picture to some extent sacred, setting him apart from the ordinary man, and giving him a more permanent existence, not only for his contempories, but also for future generations.*

There is an exceptionally fine painting of St. Theodore in the northern apse, his face expressing deep meditation. My little guide book describes it as ' one of the masterpieces of Romanian feudal portrait-painting, showing a dramatic tension '.

Among the interesting paintings in the pronaos are scenes from the martyrdom of St. George. Another is a Nativity, the shepherds wearing Moldavian dress. The prophet Elijah drives Mary and the Child, who are seated in a cart which is very similar to those used in present-day Moldavia. Elijah is dressed as an old Moldavian peasant.

The Voroneț monastery was founded by Stephen the Great in 1488 in commemoration of a defeat of the Turks in battle; enlarged by his son Petru Rareş, the originator of the exterior wall paintings of the Painted Churches; and painted in 1547.

---

* I am indebted to ' *Portraits from the Frescoes* ' by Svetislav Mandic for the above information.

Moldoviţa

As WE APPROACHED the village of Moldoviţa, I could see in the distance fortified walls and watch towers. The monastery is set in a beautiful alpine valley. Before entering it I climbed a hill and looked down. There was the church in its mantle of colours, set in the middle of emerald green lawns, guarded by twenty-foot walls and numerous watch towers. This was very different from the two previous monasteries of Humor and Voroneţ, which had no fortifications. (Plate 24.)

Descending the hill, I entered the monastery through its massive circular arched gateway which was surmounted by a tall watch tower with a spreading shingled wooden roof, topped by a crucifix.

A rich band of sculpture ran across the face of the watch tower, above which was a circular sculptured window. The walls and watch towers were made of open cast stonework, the stones attractively uneven in shape and size. As I approached the church I was surprised to see black-robed nuns, each wearing a small black hat with a black shawl partially over it. They were in charge of the monastery and looked after the guest-house.

This is the monastery built by Prince Petru Rareş, Stephen the Great's son, in 1537, its outer façades painted in 1542.

On the exterior eastern apse, which faces the entrance and continues on to the south-eastern apse, there is an immense composition vividly portraying in colour the Heavenly Church, including the Celestial Hierarchies and Earthly Church. (Plates 26, 27.)

As I passed round to the south wall, my Romanian friend looked at me expectantly to see my reaction. I said, ' All that I experienced at Voroneţ, I am experiencing again, but yet differently.'

The description in my little guide book fitted perfectly—' Adorned from top to bottom with figures, looking rather like a parchment leaf dipped in sky-blue '.

The blue background is a different blue from that of Voroneţ, the difference between ultramarine and cobalt. Out from the blue background comes The Tree of Jesse, and at the bottom of it are the Greek philosophers, Aristotle, Plato, etc. (Plate 25.) Also on this wall is a vivid realistic picture of the Siege of Constantinople by the Turks in the seventh century. The Emperor and Empress of Byzantium direct the defence of the city, aided by the Patriarch and the banner of the Virgin. As in a similar scene at Humor, the Persians are dressed as Turks; the sinners in the Voroneţ Last Judgement were also dressed as Turks. What is so strange is— why did these ' Terrible Turks ' spare these painted monasteries?

Coming round to the west front, one finds an open porch, the only example of this other

MOLDOVIŢA than the one at Humor. On the west wall of the porch there is a Last Judgement, also a St. George and the Dragon, together with St. Demetrius and the Giant. The two last scenes are depicted with dynamic movement and energy.

St. George and St. Demetrius were friends and associates in the fight against paganism.

Moldoviţa Monastery has a wonderful harmonious union of architecture, colour, surrounding walls and watch towers, integrated into the surrounding landscape of pine-clad mountains. (Plates 11, 12.)

The church itself is exceptionally well-proportioned, between its open western porch,* tower and lateral apses, and with its undulating, spreading shingled roof. The walls of the interior are profusely painted with murals; among them is a fine composition of Prince Petru Rareş surrounded by his family, presenting a model of the church to Christ enthroned. Petru Rareş' wooden chair is still preserved inside, every inch of it covered with the most delicate lace-like carving and tinted in colour.

The exterior paintings of Moldoviţa together with those of Voroneţ are the most splendid and the most beautiful examples of all the creations of Petru Rareş.

* See Humor, page 25.

Arbore

Plate 28
Arbore.
Exterior paintings 1541.
The church from the
south-west. South façade
to the right of the doorway:
The Last Judgement and
bottom row of panels depict
a standing row of figures,
among them in a group
together, the Archangel
Michael, St. George and
the Emperor Constantine.

Plate 29
Arbore.
Western façade: The
three rows of panels above
the window depict the life
of St. George. The two
rows of panels level with
the window depict the Life
of St. Demetrius. The two
rows below the window
depict the Life of
St. Nikita.

Plate 30
Arbore.
West façade top row, left
panel depicts the king
being baptized by a bishop,
behind him stands
St. George.
Centre panel: St. George at
the king's court, and right
panel; the feast. Two
central rows of panels;
Life of St. Demetrius.
Bottom panel; Life of
St. Nikita.

Arbore

COMING TO ARBORE after the splendours of Voroneţ and Moldoviţa, I viewed it with considerable disappointment due to the poor state of preservation of the murals on its southern façade, where they are usually well protected. But gradually I found its architectural simplicity, like Humor, most attractive, and as I moved further away I began to feel that there was something special about this church. (Plate 28.)

It was architecturally even simpler than Humor, having no open western porch or lateral apses, but a simple rectangle with a circular apse under its spreading roof. (See ground plan Fig. 6 on page 29.) Also the paintings were different from any of the other three churches I had seen, different in colour, position and content. For instance, there were the remains of a very interesting Last Judgement on the south façade. A hand comes down from heaven, holding the scales; the cupped hand is also holding seven seated figures dressed in yellow (souls). Slightly below to the right, Eve, dressed in a long red garment, kneels looking up to the hand in supplication; behind her is the river of blood leading to Hell. On the opposite side Adam, dressed in a long trailing white garment, also looks up to the hand in supplication. Underneath the scales are devils waiting to capture the souls on the scales. Underneath Eve, angels struggle with devils for human souls.

At the bottom of the south wall, running from the south portal, is a long procession of archangels, angels and saints moving to the eastern apse; then row by row they mount the eastern apse and disappear under the shadow of the roof, as if they were entering the church.

In the early morning, soon after sunrise, this must look quite dramatic, as the figures are mainly white (some having lost their colour), on a dark blue background.

As I moved round to the western façade I found this too was different from any of the other Painted Churches. The centre part of the wall was quite deeply-recessed under a circular arch, where the paintings were exceptionally well preserved, their wonderful colours shining bright in the evening sunlight; in fact, the sun was so low that this was the only part of the church in sunlight. (Plate 29.)

The colours were mainly red and bright green on blue backgrounds, white and pink being used as contrast. The various scenes were divided into compartments, red lines dividing them. The three rows of panels on the top half of the west façade, just above the window, have as their theme the legend of St. George.

The story reaches its climax in the magnificent double panel immediately above the window.

It had originally started with the birth and childhood, top left, but these panels have not survived. Three panels in the top row and four in the second row have survived and show the martyrdom of St. George.

Before each series of tortures, he is brought before the king, who demands that he recant his belief in Christ. Each time he refuses and he is then tortured, boiled in oil in a large tub, grilled on a wire bed over a fire (second row of three panels).

On another panel (not clear in the illustration) he fights the dragon on horseback and pierces it with his spear.

The next panel shows the victorious George standing on the subdued dragon. In front of him stands the king's daughter whom George has rescued from the dragon.

Next there is a panel showing George with the king's daughter, who leads the subdued dragon by her girdle to the king and his court. The king stands before St. George with bowed head. These panels are not visible in the illustration.

Looking at the third row of panels above the window, the panel to the left of the central double panel (Plate 30) shows the conversion of the king, who is in a church, standing before a red draped altar, opposite which stands the officiating bishop in a mantle with large crosses woven on it, while very close behind the king stands the tall majestic figure of St. George.

This panel leads to the double panel (Plate 31) which brings this part of the life of St. George to a sort of climax, the artist showing its importance by its size in comparison with all the other panels on the west façade. The double panel shows the converted king sitting on a large oval throne, holding in his two hands a double cross; and seated on either side of him are St. George and the officiating bishop. Courtiers, gorgeously attired in brilliant green, orange, and red garments, are standing on each side, row upon row. The artist achieves great skill in conveying the impression of a large number by means of receding heads. Behind the king stands his bodyguard in white pointed helmets. On a balcony above are seated the royal family.

The next panel on the immediate right shows a long table covered with a white cloth. At the head of the table is seated the king with the bishop beside him, his hand raised as if in blessing. St. George sits next to him, looking at the king.

On the table between is what looks like bread, and some of the guests at the table are holding up wine cups while looking towards the group at the top of the table. Nothing else appears on the table, but in the background are musicians. In a balcony, under a rich red oval canopy, sits the royal family. Superficially this might look like a feast, but it gives the impression of a spiritual rite. The illustration does not show the colours correctly; these, as in the preceding panel, should be rich reds, oranges and greens.

The next panel to the right, not visible in the illustration, shows St. George on a white horse, with a group of horsemen behind him, setting forth to Nicomedia, the Eastern capital, to plead the Christian cause before the Emperor Diocletian.

The story of St. George's fight with the dragon is found in Jacques de Voragine's *The Golden Legend*, written in the thirteenth century.

He tells us that when the Emperor Diocletian persecuted the Christians, St. George retired from the army to support them and was on his way to the Emperor to plead their cause when, while passing through Silene (near modern Beirut), he met the dragon, which had been terrorising the whole neighbourhood. ' And when he came nigh the city, he envenomed the

the devil in dragon form standing by her left foot. The whole posture is very dynamic. My Romanian friend rushed me into the church to show me this painting. (Plate 32.)

St. Marina, who was known in the West as St. Margaret of Antioch, was one of the most popular saints in the later Middle Ages.

In the reign of the Emperor Diocletian, a pagan priest of Antioch in Pisidia had a daughter Marina (Margaret) who was said to have been brought up as a Christian by her nurse. The prefect Olybius, attracted by her beauty, was determined to possess her, but she rejected him and he denounced her as a Christian and she was imprisoned. During her captivity Satan is said to have appeared to her in the form of a dragon, and to have contrived to swallow her whole. She was saved from a horrible death by the Cross she held in her hand, which caused the dragon to disgorge her unharmed. Subsequently she was beheaded.

In the Victoria and Albert Museum there is a limestone figure of St. Marina (Margaret) and the dragon dating from the sixteenth century, depicting St. Marina standing on the winged dragon with hands together in prayer. She looks down at the dragon, who looks up at her, with part of her garment in his mouth.

It is said in another story that Marina's father was a monk in Bithynia and kept his daughter in the monastery with him, disguised as a boy. On his death she went on living undetected in the monastery.

History relates that Jeanne d'Arc believed that St. Marina, together with St. Catherine, appeared to her constantly and advised her in all her undertakings. St. Marina's Calendar day is July 20th.

It is interesting to note that St. George and St. Marina appeared together in mediaeval times in the Norwich annual St. George's Day processions, which were thus unique in honouring two saints instead of one, St. Marina taking the place of the princess. It was a very splendid festival in which she and St. George rode together, magnificently dressed in crimson, on horses richly draped in red and black velvet. With them went the dragon. Accompanied by the mayor and aldermen in their scarlet robes, they rode through the streets to the cathedral, where a service was held. Later they went to a nearby wood, where, as an old document of 1408 records, the traditional battle between St. George and the dragon was re-enacted.

prolong the overpast rule of Gabriel, so George worked to ensure and implement the dawning rule of Michael . . . . From the Crusades onwards the story of St. George shows him growing into his present spiritual leadership of England, and at the same time beginning to lay the groundwork of his future spiritual leadership of Russia.'*

The old imperial coat of arms of the Russian tsars depicts the red double eagle of the Byzantine Empire. On its wings it bears the arms of all the peoples it has conquered. In the centre, as if protecting the heart of Russia, is a large shield showing the Archangel Michael conquering the dragon. The folk-spirit of Russia is represented in the heart of the eagle.

Since St. George can be considered as the earthly servant of the Archangel Michael, the picture in the centre of this coat of arms can also represent St. George conquering the dragon; this is felt very strongly in the soul of the Russian people. In the future this will be understood more clearly. Russia then will be Holy Russia.

' And there was war in heaven: Michael and his angels fought against the dragon; and the dragon fought and his angels, and prevailed not; neither was their place found anymore in heaven. And the great dragon was cast out, that old serpent, called the Devil, and Satan, which deceiveth the whole world: he was cast out into the earth, and his angels were cast out with him.' (*Revelations* 12: 7–9.)

The dragon expelled from Heaven still continues his war against man. The serpent is sometimes portrayed at the foot of the Cross to signify that its evil power can be overcome with the help of Christ.

St. George's Day, April 23rd, is also Shakespeare's birthday, which is celebrated at Stratford-on-Avon by people from all over the world. Shakespeare was born on St. George's Day in 1564 and died on St. George's Day in 1616. It is perhaps significant that this greatest of Englishmen entered and left this world at Stratford, right in the heart of England, on the very day of the festival of England's Guardian Saint—St. George.

Returning to the Arbore murals, below the Life of St. George, on two rows of panels centred on the window and extending to the edges of the recess, is depicted the life of St. Demetrius (see Plate 30). The centre of his cult was in Salonika. The story told there was that he was a local man who was martyred for preaching Christianity in the reign of the Emperor Maximilian and he became famous as a warrior saint linked with St. George. They are shown together on many icons.

The bottom two rows below the window, also extending to the edges of the recess, depict the life of St. Nikita, who was a Goth and who was martyred in A.D. 372 by being burnt to death. His body was taken to Asia, to Mopsuestia in Cilicia, and his memory held in honour all over the East. *The Book of the Painters* from Mount Athos instructs that St. Nikita be painted as a young saint with a beard, to resemble Christ in appearance, and that he should be standing in the fire that was to destroy his physical body.

One of the paintings in the interior is very striking. Saint Marina is shown, in a red under-robe with a bright green mantle covering her head and shoulders, raising a hammer to strike

---

* *Michael, St. George and the Holy Sophia.* (The Golden Blade, 1954.)

The early fourth century *Martyrdom of St. George* which proclaims itself as written by Pasi-krates, George's faithful servant and an eye-witness of his martyrdom, tells us that after the first day of St. George's torture, Christ comes down to him in the night, comforting him and saying: ' Be strong and of good cheer, beloved George. Thou shalt die three times, and I will raise thee up again; but after the fourth time I myself will come upon a cloud and will take thee away to the place of safe-keeping which I have prepared for thy holy dwelling. Be strong and fear not, for I am with thee.'

After St. George's first death upon the wheel of knives, his bones are thrown into a deep pit outside the city; and ' that night there came a great earthquake, and the mountains split asunder suddenly; and Michael blew with his trumpet, and behold the Lord came upon His chariot of the Cherubim, and stood on the edge of the pit. And He said to the Archangel Michael: ' Go down into the pit and gather together the bones of My son George.' And Michael went down into the pit and put together the holy body of St. George, and the Lord took his hand, saying: ' O George, My beloved, behold, the hand which formed Adam the first man is about to create thee anew.' And the Lord breathed upon his face, and filled him again with life; and He embraced him, and went up to heaven again with His holy angels.'

The resurrected George was killed a second time and a second time Christ came and raised him from the dead. A third time George was killed and a third time Christ came and raised him from the dead. Then came the day of George's final death. 'And the Lord said to the Blessed George: " Blessed art thou this day, George My beloved, for I have made ready for thee seven crowns of glory in the hands of My Father, and He will place them upon thy head this day." And the soldiers took off his holy head, and there came forth from it blood and milk.'*

After St. George's beheading, his servants Pasikrates, Lukios and Kirennios ' joined the head of the saint to his body ' and the body was taken to Lydda and buried, and its burial place became a place of pilgrimage. The Emperor Diocletian, urged on by Galerius, was preparing to embark to destroy this shrine, when ' behold, the holy Archangel Michael and St. George came down from heaven, and over-turned under him the throne on which he sat, saying, ' Now thy dominion is passed away and is given to Constantine, who is more excellent than thou a thousand times".'†

St. George was aged thirty-three when he was beheaded. Diocletian abdicated two years after St. George's death, and a year later his successor Constantine Chlorus died and his son Constantine the Great became emperor of the West.

The martyrdom of his comrade St. George had so powerful an effect on the new emperor that he brought Christianity exoterically into the Roman Empire. He himself was not baptised until the eve of his own death, thirty-three years after St. George's martyrdom.

So St. George becomes the champion of Christianity, and as the Roman Empire begins to break up, ' other impulses begin to appear; that championing of Christianity against heathen-dom, with which his martyrdom is bound up, takes a new, decisive turn. It emerges in sharp clarity as a championing of the Cross against the Crescent . . . . As Mahomet worked to

---

* In *The Golden Blade,* 1953 and 1954.
† *Ibid.*

people with his breath; and therefore the people of the city gave to him every day two sheep to feed him, because he should do no harm to the people; and when the sheep failed, there was a man taken and a sheep '. Then lots were cast, and the lot fell on the king's daughter, and while the princess was standing near the place where the dragon lived, St. George passed by on horseback, and, seeing the girl was weeping, spoke to her.

Then the dragon appeared, and St. George, making the sign of the Cross, fought with him and wounded him with his spear. He directed the princess to tie her girdle round the dragon's neck. 'When she had done so the dragon followed her as it had been a meek beast and debonair '. As they led the dragon into the king's city everybody was terrified. ' Then St. George said to them, Doubt ye nothing; without more, believe ye in God, Jesu Christ, and do ye to be baptized; I shall slay the dragon. Then the king was baptized and all his people; and St. George slew the dragon and smote off his head. After this slaying he went on to the imperial court at Nicomedia '.

This tale from *The Golden Legend* took a strong hold on the minds and hearts of the people of the Middle Ages and has continued in one form or another into recent times. In a study, *Michael, St. George and the Holy Sophia** the writer says of it: ' The conquest of the dragon follows the path of purification of man's lower nature. In the princess live the pure, innocent forces of the soul; her girdle, tied about the neck of the dragon when once St. George has subdued it, has the power of turning it into a meek beast and debonair. Therefore it is always stressed that she is a pure virgin. That the dragon was seen as destroying both innocence and true manhood is indicated in its devouring daily one lamb and one man. In old paintings of St. George fighting the dragon, a lamb frequently nestles besides the praying princess '.

In the same study, details from fourth and fifth century Coptic texts in the Bodleian and Vatican libraries give the story the following background: St. George was born in the year A.D. 270 at Militene (Cappadocia). and received his military training under the Emperor Diocletian, serving under him in the Egyptian campaign of 295, and under Galerius in the Persian War which followed. In both campaigns his comrade-in-arms was Constantine, whom Diocletian had taken into the army as hostage when in 293 he had raised the youth's father, Constantine Chlorus, together with Galerius, to the rank of Caesar (subordinate Emperor). During the first fourteen years of Diocletian's reign (284–298), the Christian Church had flourished unmolested; but in 298, incited by Galerius, Diocletian issued the decree that all soldiers must take part in the non-Christian sacrificial rites which was to bring about St. George's martyrdom; and in 303, still under the influence of Galerius, he ordered the destruction of all Christian churches and professing Christians throughout the Empire. In the Eastern Church nearly forty thousand Christians were slain in this sudden purge; in the West, over ten thousand in Caerleon-on-Usk alone.

This was the background against which George Tarbinus (George the Tribune) came to Nicomedia, the capital of the Eastern Empire, and before Galerius and the sixty-nine judges who sat with him in the judgment hall of the great Roman Basilica there, boldly proclaimed: ' I am a Christian! ' From that day St. George's martyrdom commenced.

---

* In *The Golden Blade,* 1953 and 1954.

Sucevița

Plate 34
Sucevița.
The church from the south.

Plate 37
Suceviţa.
South façade: Tree of Jesse.
Lower register: The Greek
Philosophers Plato,
Pythagoras, Aristotle, and
Sophocles.

Plate 38
Sucevita.
South lateral apse:
Procession of Saints.

Plate 39
Sucevița.
Southern and eastern
apses: Procession of Saints.

Plate 41
Sucevița.
Porch: St. John the
Baptist.

Dragomirna

Plate 42
Dragomirna
Monastery. From the
east (1609).

Plate 43
Dragomirna
Monastery. Sculptured
steeple and the eastern
apse.

Sucevița

My first sight of Sucevița was when I was high up in the mountains. I could see the monastery nestling in its alpine valley away in the distance.

As I approached the monastery through the village I could see two gentle sloping hills to the north and south overlooking the monastery. I climbed up the southern hill and looked down on the monastery beneath me.

It was most dramatic, with the church standing there in the middle, surrounded by its massive walls and glowing like a jewel in the sunlight. These protecting walls are eighteen feet high and nine feet thick, with towers marking the four corners. The south-western and south-eastern towers are octagonal. (Plate 33.)

This is the last of the Painted Churches, being built in 1584 by the Movila family and painted between 1602 and 1604.

The new century was to produce a new style of painting and architecture, as we shall see when we consider the Dragomirna Monastery.

I entered Sucevița monastery through a massive arched gateway above which was a well-preserved painting. Above is a small chapel. The door was opened by a black-robed nun.

Owing to its later date and high walls, the exterior paintings are the best preserved of all the Painted Churches, the north façade being as well-preserved as the south façade. Strangely enough there are no paintings left on the west façade. The colour scheme is different, too. Green and indigo predominate, with red and yellow coming next in importance, while white sets off the other colours.

The church architecturally has a general resemblance to Moldovița, but it is not so well-proportioned; this is partially due to two porches on the north and south at the western end of the church, a novel element from Wallachia which was to influence churches in the seventeenth century. But here at Sucevița they are rather bulky, and break the harmonious proportions of the church. (Plate 34.)

The exterior paintings enhance the architecture. Although the themes echo those of the other churches, they are nevertheless different, mainly as a result of the colour scheme.

On the south façade there is an extensive Tree of Jesse but on an indigo background. At the bottom are the Greek philosophers—Aristotle, Plato, Pythagoras and Sophocles, who are very vigorously drawn and coloured. The early Church Fathers considered such Greek philosophers as among the prophets announcing the coming of Christ. (Plates 35, 37.)

The rest of the south façade shows the Hymn of the Holy Virgin. The Virgin is pictured alone in a mountain landscape. The three Magi on horseback are also vigorously drawn and coloured.

The two porches have scenes from the life of St. John the New, patron saint of Moldavia. There are fourteen panels culminating in the carrying of the Saint's relics to Suceava and a panel of St. George engaged with the dragon.

It is very interesting comparing the way the lives of St. George and St. John the New are shown on the different churches, each one having an individuality of its own.

Inside the porch there is a very strange painting of St. John the Baptist,* with wings. (Plate 41.)

Along the lateral apse and round the eastern apse, the Procession of Saints wends its way. Here the green backgrounds are very effective, especially in the upper scenes. (Plates 36, 38, 39.) The green continues round to the north lateral apse. Now we come to the main part of the north façade. This wall is covered by a very unusual composition, The Ladder of Sin, which shows a ladder set diagonally across the wall. All along the right side of the ladder are rows of angels, leaning forward towards the ladder, dressed in red with golden haloes. On the ladder are many souls ascending. Each rung of the ladder represents a mortal sin. To the left of the ladder are many horrible-looking devils with horns, some with many heads, who clutch the souls as they fall from the ladder. Those who have trodden on the rung of the mortal sin they have committed are dragged down to Hell. There are some black devils who carry white parcels containing the sins of the souls ascending the ladder.

Above the highest rung Christ stretches out His hand to welcome to Heaven those who safely make the perilous climb.

Here, as in the other churches, are angels with spears trying to protect even those sinful souls who have been forced from the ladder. All the colours of this composition are very effectively painted on an indigo background. (Plate 40.)

Inside the church there are extremely impressive scenes of the lives of all the saints of the Eastern Orthodox Church depicted on the anti-nave walls. There are 365 of them, dressed in a great variety of costumes belonging to different periods of history, and depicted against many backgrounds—citadels, walls, mountains, even seascapes. The scenes are always full of life and activity, realistic in one sense, yet the painter has managed to weave a mystical mood throughout the series.

The Orthodox Calendar is, in its framework, the same as the Western Calendar; that is to say, it is built up around the great festivals which are common to the whole of Christendom, Easter being the chief of all. There is no Trinity Sunday, the first Sunday after Whitsuntide being used for the commemoration of All Saints. There is also no season of Advent, but every day is marked by the commemoration of a saint or saints, varying in different parts of the Orthodox world, as there are many local saints, such as St. John the New in Romania. Practically none of the minor saints belong to both Western and Orthodox calendars, the outstanding exception being St. George, who is highly venerated in the East as the Great Martyr whose spiritual presence continues from early Christian times to the present and on into the future.

---

* See Foreword, page 11.

44

There is a very striking votive painting on two walls, on a blue background with gold stars, depicting a long procession of the ruling Movila family, founders of the monastery. In it are five young princesses, with crowns, behind their mother; Prince Movila, with his very young son, hands a model of the church to the seated Christ; and the Virgin Mary stands beside the Christ in the same position as St. George at Voroneț.

The walls of these Painted Churches give in dynamic pictures the stories of the lives of the saints, fabulous events rejected by our modern consciousness. But during the Middle Ages and in the Orthodox Church as late as the sixteenth century, they were believed and accorded the same veneration as were these saints' icons.

Eleanor Merry writes in her book *The Flaming Door:** 'All myths, sagas and legends are like a shimmering veil of many colours, stirred now and then by the winds of our desires, but still hiding from most of us that Council of the Wise seated at the Round Table of the Stars, who once painted, on the moving veil, the bright pictures of fairy-tale and myth with the breath of their immortal Words. But between us and them lies the gulf of our arrogance and the mists of our unbelief.'

Eleanor Merry in *Easter: The Legends and the Fact*† writes further: ' The age which we now rather proudly call the " age of science " dawned in the early part of the fifteenth century. And its approach, showing itself in the general culture and in individual persons, was clouded by a certain fear or premonition: a fear that a more exact science of Nature—a physical science —must inevitably at last plunge mankind into a denial of the spiritual. It is an interesting truth that what are really the important factors in making of history very often disappear into legend, and in disappearing into legend their real traces become obscured and are finally disbelieved in. This is the reason why it is so difficult to trace with exactitude the lives of certain important people—who were really representative of progressive or destructive forces.'

This is very relevant when we consider Klingsor, leader of the anti-Grail forces in Sicily and Spain, as connected with the destructive forces,‡ and St. George as representing the progressive stream.

Perhaps it is the destiny of these five churches to break down the wall of our unbelief, and it is through Art that this can most easily be done, because it appeals more to the heart than to the intellect.

This brings us to the end of the Painted Churches and the beginning of a new century. Sucevița has many pointers to the seventeenth century. But it is surprising that these Painted Churches should have come into being and ended in such a short period as sixty-five years.

* Eleanor C. Merry. *The Flaming Door.* New Knowledge Books, London.
† Eleanor C. Merry. *Easter: The Legends and the Facts.* New Knowledge Books, London.
‡ Rudolf Steiner. *Mysteries of the East and Christianity.* Rudolf Steiner Press, London.

A new era : Dragomirna Monastery
(Mitocu Dragomirnei)

THE ROAD FROM Suceava came to an end among pine forests and rolling hills where, above the trees, rose the high walls and watch towers of the Dragomirna Monastery. Passing round the south walls, I climbed a small hill on the other side and looked out across a lake to the soaring church in the midst of its massive ramparts, reflecting themselves in the water. (Plate 42.) This was indeed a beautiful setting. Built by Bishop Crimca, Metropolitan of Moldavia, it was his masterpiece, bringing new elements of the Christian impulse into the seventeenth century through art.

A worthy successor to the Painted Churches!

Passing through the massive gateway, I saw the Moldavian coat of arms above the archway.

The composition is quite remarkable with its forms containing cosmic and esoteric secrets.

Four parts of a circle form a cross framing a long-necked auroch* carrying the six-pointed star between its horns. Seen from the front the circular arms of the cross contain, on the left, the face of the sun with rays and, on the right, in profile the face of the moon, emerging from its crescent. In the bottom part of the circle is a Byzantine cross with a slanting cross-bar from a Russian tradition that Christ was lame,† and the characters of the inscription on the four parts of the cross are beautifully carved.

I entered the monastery.

The church was fantastic, seemingly soaring up to heaven, twice as high as any other church in Moldavia, the effect of great height being increased by its slender width with no lateral apses to break the tremendous upward thrust of the walls.

Rising high above the roof is a sculptured steeple, lavish in its intricate carving, almost like embroidery. (Plate 43.)

The massive belfry and corner watch towers contrast strongly with the soaring Gothic proportions of the church. The plainness of the exterior walls is relieved by an unusual sculptured twisted-rope motif, which runs round the centre of the whole church.

The interior of the church is different from the churches of the sixteenth century because it

---

* Aurochs were huge wild cattle that formerly inhabited central Europe. They probably survived in the Polish forests up to the end of the 16th century, and were between 7 and 8 ft. high and black to reddish in colour.

† The Holy Shroud was preserved in Constantinople from the fourth to the early thirteenth century. (In 1204, when the armies of the Fourth Crusade took Constantinople, the shroud was sent to France.) The shadowy imprint on it was therefore venerated in Eastern Christianity for centuries before the Shroud came to the West. In this imprint the right leg appears shorter than the left. The missionaries from Constantinople who spread Christianity in Russia taught that Christ was a cripple, suffering thus for the sins of Men. Details are given in *The True Likeness* by R. W. Hynk. (Sheed and Ward Ltd.)

Fig. 8. The Moldavian Coat of Arms.

ends with a polygonal apse instead of the usual rounded one. The twisted-rope motif of the exterior is also used inside very effectively.

The steeple, which is octagonal on the outside and circular inside, rises over the nave and rests on four large archways, enhanced by the twisted-rope motif and supported by massive corbels.

The paintings in the nave, like the architecture, are the result of new ideas coming into being in the new century, ideas which were foreshadowed in the Sucevița Monastery and developed dramatically in the architecture at Dragomirna. So the Byzantine impulse goes through another transformation.

I arrived back in Bucharest from Suceava in a violent thunderstorm; the wind was driving the rain with great force, and outside the station was a seething mass of people trying to get taxis. After half an hour I was reconciling myself to spending the night at the station when a lady who had been in my carriage, but had not spoken to me, came up to me and said she would get me a car. She went out into the pouring rain and came back with a car—another unexpected good Samaritan.

So my pilgrimage to Romania came to an end. I call it a pilgrimage because I felt it was very special Christian impulses that brought the unique Painted Churches into being. Though this was during such a short period in history, they will be handed down to posterity. Great works of art have always a message for the future.

Note on the Voroneţ Signs of the Zodiac

THESE SIGNS DEPICTED at the top of the west façade above the Last Judgement at Voroneţ have a special interest due to the animals of the Zodiac having fishes' tails. The Goat is shown as a horse with a single horn, like a unicorn, while the hindquarters become the tail of a fish. The usual Zodiacal sign of the Fishes here gives place to a seated figure in a shell, holding two fishes across his body.

Unfortunately this interesting and unusual Zodiac was too high for me to photograph in detail, but it can be seen at the top of the wall on Plate 18.

The Fish is an important Christian symbol. This is because the five Greek letters forming the word 'fish' are the initial letters of the five words: 'Jesus, Christ, God's Son, Saviour.' This symbol is often found inscribed on early Christian slabs.

In *The Catacombs** are many illustrations of the Fish used thus as a symbol of Christianity. One shows two fishes and some loaves, symbols of the eucharistic food; another (dated 2nd and 3rd century), a Fish carrying a basket containing bread and wine; a third (a mosaic from S. Vitale, Ravenna, dating from the middle of the sixth century) depicts the Holy Meal, with Christ and the twelve disciples at a round table, and on the table bread and two fishes.

The author's comment: ' The early Christians must have felt inwardly quickened when they gazed at the representation of the Fish. The picture awakened the sensation of eternally progressing, streaming, surging life. In designating Christ by the picture of the Fish, the principle of progress as the necessary enemy of all stagnation and reaction was expressed. The water of life is the element in which the Fish lives. To be united with Christ meant to participate in this flowing, rejuvenating life.'

The Zodiac itself belongs to this sphere of the water of life — it is, in a sense, the spiritual background out of which physical creation is ' spoken forth.'

I have seen fish-tailed animals reminiscent of this Voroneţ Zodiac in another church, some four hundred years earlier — on the twelfth century painted Romanesque ceiling in St. Martin's church at Zillis in Switzerland. The panels of this ceiling represent the life of Christ, but on the panels of the outer border are shown a bear, a unicorn, an elephant, a hound, all with the tails of fishes. These fish-tailed animals suggest man's future redemption of the animal world through the flowing, rejuvenating life Christ, the Fish, is bringing to Man, for we know from St. Paul that man has to be (in Novalis' phrase) the Messiah of Nature.

A friend to whom I sent the illustration of the Voroneţ Last Judgement with the descriptive

---

* *The Catacombs*. Pictures from The Life of Early Christianity. By Emil Bock and Robert Goebel. Edited and enlarged by Alfred Heideneich. The Christian Community Press.

49

text wrote back — ' Reading your description of this wonderful Last Judgement, the picture I have is of a descent from God the Creator in the Heights through successive panels to Man and his deeds on earth and his reaping of their harvest in the life after death, God is surrounded in the sea of Cosmic ether by the twelve mighty constellations — the fish-tailed Zodiac signs — which together speak forth the being of Man; with Christ as Sun-Being we are already a step nearer the earth; with the Virgin Mary and St. John the Baptist, we (and He) have reached it. The prevalence of angels reminds us that even the Zodiac is a picturing-forth of Heavenly hierarchies. This whole Last Judgement must have been a powerful theme for meditation.'

Water-Colour Paintings

Plate 7
Wooden Church,
Maramureş, Transylvania.

Plate 9
Voronet.
The church,
south-west. Exterior
paintings 1547
(Water-colour).

Plate 12
Moldoviţa.
The church, south-east
(Water-colour).

Bibliography

Romania. A Complete Guide. Peter Latham. (The Garnstone Press, 1967.)

Arbore. 50 Illustrations in Colour. (Verlag Meridiane, Bucarest 1968.)

Voroneţ. 59 Illustrations in Colour. (Verlag Meridiane, Bucarest 1969.)

Voroneţ (Historical Monuments Pocket Guide) by Petru Comarnescu. (Meridiane Publishing House, Bucharest 1964.)

The Humor Monastery (Historical Monuments Pocket Guide) by Stefan Bals. (Meridiane Publishing House, Bucharest 1965.)

Moldoviţa Monastery (Historical Monuments Pocket Guide) by Corina Nicolesco. (Meridiane Publishing House, Bucharest 1967.)

The Suceviţa Monastery (Historical Monuments Pocket Guide) by Maria Ana Musicescu. (Meridiane Publishing House, Bucharest 1967.)

The Dragomirna Monastery (Historical Monuments Pocket Guide) by Teodora Voinescu and Razvan Theodorescu. (Meridiane Publishing House, Bucharest 1965.)

Romanian Invitation by William Forwood. (Garnstone Press 1968.)

Christianity and Communism by Charles Davy. (Threefold Commonwealth Research Group.)

Religion in the U.S.S.R. Editor Robert Conquest. (Bodley Head.)

In God's Underground by Richard Wurmbrand. (W. H. Allen, London 1968.)

The Flaming Door by Eleanor C. Merry. (New Knowledge Books, London.)

A History of Architecture (On the Comparative Method) by Sir Banister Fletcher (B. T. Batsford, Ltd. London.)

The Golden Legend by Jacques de Voragine.

Martyrdom of St. George by Pasikrates.

Meditations On the Signs of the Zodiac by John Jocelyn. (Rudolf Steiner Publications, New-York 1970.)

Europe: A New Picture by Maria Schindler. (Michael Press, London 1972.)

Index

52

MUSIC: ITS OCCULT BASIS AND HEALING VALUE
Edited by Lionel Stebbing

102 contributions on every important aspect of music and healing by writers on Rudolf Steiner's Spiritual Science. Bruno Walter writes: " My whole being is rejuvenated, and I feel a strong, rewarding influence also in regard to the musician within me ". " Much wisdom and inspiration ".—Anthroposophical Quarterly. £1.50

THE MYSTERY-WISDOM OF COLOUR
by Gladys Mayer

The creative power and healing value of colour. With 29 illustrations in full colour. £1.25

COMMON AILMENTS AND THEIR NATURAL REMEDIES *(Formerly " The Art of Healing ")*
Edited by A. E. Abbot (Rudolf Steiner's indications) 30p.

HONEY AS HEALER
Edited by Lionel Stebbing 20p.

ENCYCLOPAEDIA OF NUMBERS: THEIR ESSENCE AND MEANING
by A. E. Abbott

A treasury of esoteric teaching on numbers and rhythms in human life, with data on famous mathematicians, philosophers, occultists who have written on numbers. 524 pages. £3.25

SPIRITUAL KNOWLEDGE, THE REALITY AND ITS SHADOW
by Eleaner C. Merry

An outstanding book on the relation of the living to the dead, on life after death, the truth about spiritualism, mediumship, automatic writing, astral projection, etc. 90p.

THE ASCENT OF MAN
by Eleanor C. Merry

77 illustrations, many rare; 36 plates in full colour. This fascinating, profusely illustrated book deals with man's changing consciousness through the ages. Bible Wisdom; Ancient Indian Mysteries; Mysteries of Persia; Egypt, Greece, Hibernia; Edda and Kalevala; Gospels; Gnosis; Middle Ages; Renaissance; Modern Times. This book strikes like a dazzling searchlight across the horizon of esoteric advancement. A treasure of spiritual teaching which sheds unexpected light on our present and future as well. 462 pages. £3.15

A NEW IMPULSE IN ART
by Arild Rosenkrantz

Since the beginning of this century Art has experienced increasingly revolutionary phases. In this enlightening and stimulating book the author deals with the problems which have led to so much conflict and chaos today. He shows that true art is the instrument by means of which the spiritual world can speak to man and the channel for the inflow of vivifying spiritual power. With 6 colour plates. £1.65

THE APOCALYPSE OF ST. JOHN
by Emil Bock

Shows how the message of this great esoteric work is vital to our age.

£1.05

DICTIONARY OF THE OCCULT SCIENCES
by Lionel Stebbing

1,370 definitions and explanations relating to esoteric, religious, mystical and philosophical teachings throughout the ages, alphabetically arranged. 252 pages.

£1.60

THE PHILOSOPHY OF SPIRITUAL ACTIVITY
by Rudolf Steiner

Entirely new translation by Rita Stebbing. Introduced by Hugo S. Bergmann, Ph.D. With Steiner's " Truth and Knowledge ".

Paperback £2.00

INITIATION AND MEDITATION
by Arnold Freeman

What Rudolf Steiner says about how to meditate and the modern meaning of Initiation.

60p.

MEDITATIVE PRAYERS FOR TODAY
by Adam Bittleston

35p.

CHYMICAL WEDDING OF CHRISTIAN ROSENKREUTZ
Story and Commentary by I. Wyatt and M. Bennell

48p.

CLAIRVOYANCE
by 29 Authorities. Edited by A. E. Abbot

35p.

REINCARNATION
by Guenther Wachsmuth

Standard work on Reincarnation and how destiny works.

£2.30

THE SECRETS OF NUMBERS
by Lionel Stebbing

A fascinating introduction to the working of Numbers in human life.

43p.

THE NUMBER SEVEN
by A. E. Abbot

The spiritual significance of the number seven in human life.

30p.

THE NUMBER THREE
by A. E. Abbot

The spiritual significance of the number three in human life.

30p.

RECOMMENDED BOOKS

THE GREAT INITIATES
by Edouard Schuré

Now in print again, this occult classic, born of the author's personal experience, is so dynamic that its message can transform your life.

£4.35

CHRISTIANITY AS MYSTICAL FACT
by Rudolf Steiner

Deals with the spiritual path from the ancient pre-Christian Mysteries to their fulfilment in the Mystery of Golgotha and shows the importance of the Deed of Christ for human and world development.   £3.45

COSMIC MEMORY
by Rudolf Steiner

The pre-history of Earth and Man. Originally entitled " Atlantis and Lemuria ".   £3.45

THE EVOLUTION OF MANKIND
by Guenther Wachsmuth

The significance of cosmic influences that play into human history. 108 illustrations.   £2.60

KNOWLEDGE OF THE HIGHER WORLDS
by Rudolf Steiner

Gives detailed methods for the cultivating and development of spiritual organs of perception which lie dormant in all of us. 160 pp.   70p.

A GUIDE TO OCCULT BOOKS
by A. E. Abbot

Deals with 200 subjects relating to the Esoteric and Sacred Writings of the ages. There are 1,200 Author-entries, 1,630 Book-entries and 185 Cross references.   35p.

THEOSOPHY OF THE ROSICRUCIAN
by Rudolf Steiner

The age-old wisdom of the Rosicrucians presented in modern terms, in harmony with contemporary needs.   14 lectures.   £1.05

THE THREE YEARS
by Emil Bock

An outstanding work on the Life of Christ.   £1.05

OUTSTANDING BOOKS

By ELEANOR C. MERRY

ART: ITS OCCULT BASIS AND HEALING VALUE

This book shows that true Art is the instrument by means of which the spiritual world can speak to man and the channel for the inflow of vivifying spiritual power. It shows that artistic activity is important for man. It is needed as a healing force against the unbalanced materialistic philosophy of modern life. With 9 plates in full colour. Prospectus free.
£2.00

THE FLAMING DOOR

In this book E. C. Merry shows that the mystical development of ancient Celtic Mythology is deeply connected with the foundations of Christianity. She points out how the gradual metamorphoses of the pre-Christian Mysteries of the West may be traced in their effects *even in the world problems of our own time*. With 66 illustrations, 10 in full Colour. 432 pages. Prospectus free.
£2.50

THE YEAR AND ITS FESTIVALS

In this important book for the student of esoteric wisdom, and for the lover of Nature, Eleanor C. Merry deals with the spiritual aspects of Day, Night, the Week, Month and Year and its Four Seasons. The reader will find that the Year takes on a deep significance far beyond the materialistic aspect so common today.
50p.

GOETHE'S APPROACH TO COLOUR

Extracts from Goethe's out-of-print " Theory of Colour " and " Moral Effects of Colours ", translated by Eleanor C. Merry.
63p.

EASTER, THE LEGENDS AND THE FACT

Some of the chapter headings indicate the important esoteric content of this book: Sun, Moon and Earth—The Holy Grail—The Story of Parsifal —The Legend of Faust—Easter and Michaelmas—Fixing the Date for Easter, a threat to the esoteric content of the Easter festival. With two colour plates.
90p.

REMEMBERED GODS AND OTHER POEMS

A collection of fifty-four poems. These poems are refreshingly simple, yet underlying this simplicity is a deep esoteric content. They appeal to readers who are not usually interested in poetry.
25p.

See also under Recommended Books

NEW KNOWLEDGE BOOKS
28 Dean Road,
London, N.W.2.

Postage extra.   Complete Catalogue sent on request.

RUDOLF STEINER'S MESSAGE TO MANKIND
by Arnold Freeman   25p.

RUDOLF STEINER ENTERS MY LIFE
by Friedrich Rittelmeyer

> A rich personal impression. Many proofs of Steiner's seership. 150 pages.
> 90p.

THE CREATIVE POWER OF COLOUR
by H. Boos-Hamburger

> This basic course in Colour and Painting includes: The Basis of Goethe's
> Colour Theory—Physiological Colours— Rudolf Steiner points to Spirit
> in Form and Colour—Moral and Spiritual experience of Colour—Goethe's
> Colour Circle—Steiner's Colour Circle—Image and Lustre Colours.
> 66 illustrations in colour.   £1.25

THE REALITY IN WHICH WE LIVE
by F. W. Zeylmans van Emmichoven, M.D.

> An outstanding new introduction to Rudolf Steiner's work. Life, Death
> and Resurrection; Preparation for the Advent of Christ in ancient
> civilisations; The Ministry of Jesus Christ; The Resurrection; Esoteric
> Streams in Christianity; Goethe; Christ as Reality in Science, Art,
> Religion and Social Practice; Reincarnation and Destiny; Christ in
> Man and Mankind.   £1.30

GOETHE'S THEORY OF COLOUR
Applied by Maria Schindler

> In this book the reader is introduced to the secrets of colours and their
> living spiritual reality. Colours are shown as real forces which speak to
> our sensations and feelings and imprint their dynamic qualities upon our
> inner life. This is an illustrated text book, with graduated exercises leading
> the student direct into the living realm of Colour. 41 plates in full colour.
> 252 pages.   £2.50

OCCULT SCIENCE, AN OUTLINE
by Rudolf Steiner

> Essential to an understanding of man's origin, mission and final goal.
> Exercises in spiritual development; life after death; the course of man's
> life; higher regions of the spiritual world; dreams and their significance;
> how to acquire spiritual knowledge; events and beings of the Spiritual
> World. 326 pages.   Cloth £1.50

THEOSOPHY—Supersensible Knowledge of the World and the Destination of Man
by Rudolf Steiner

> Basic book, essential to an understanding of Rudolf Steiner's Spiritual
> Science.   50p.

ROSICRUCIANISM AND MODERN INITIATION
by Rudolf Steiner

> Mystery Centres of the Middle Ages. The influence of the Rosicrucian
> stream in the spiritual life of humanity in the West.   90p.

RUSSIA, PAST, PRESENT AND FUTURE
Compiled by John Fletcher

An Anthology dealing with occult aspects of Russia. Sir Winston Churchill once described Russia as "a conundrum inside an enigma". In their relationships with Russia the nations of Western Europe have always felt the sense of something perplexing, of almost entirely incalculable forces. One of the greatest dangers of our times lies in the failure to understand the Russian character and conflicting forces that exist in the Russian soul. The writers of these articles bring new light on these conflicts and they look beyond the troubles of the present towards a future when hidden Christian forces will bear fruit in the Russian soul. With 94 illustrations, 51 in colour. £2.50

Postage extra. Complete Catalogue sent on request

NEW KNOWLEDGE BOOKS

28 Dean Road,

London, N.W.2.

NEW KNOWLEDGE PAPERBACKS

Based on Rudolf Steiner's Spiritual Science

THE WISDOM IN FAIRY TALES
by Ursula Grahl 25p.

THE BRITISH: THEIR PSYCHOLOGY AND DESTINY
by Dr. W. J. Stein 40p.

THE MYSTERIES OF THE ROSE-CROSS
by George Adams, M.A. 21p.

THE HANDICAPPED CHILD
by Dr. Karl König 10p.

UNDERSTANDING YOUR CHILD
by Lionel Stebbing 45p.

HOW TO HELP YOUR GROWING CHILD
by Ursula Grahl 20p.

THE HUMAN SOUL IN SLEEPING & WAKING
by F. W. Zeylmans v. Emmichoven, M.D. 11p.

BEHIND THE VEILS OF DEATH AND SLEEP
by Gladys Mayer 20p.

DESTINY AND FREEDOM
by Herman Poppelbaum 10p.

TRUTH AND ERROR IN ASTROLOGY
by Dr. Hermann Poppelbaum 11p.

THE SECRETS OF NUMBERS
by Lionel Stebbing 43p.

Postage extra. Complete List of Paperbacks sent on request.

NEW KNOWLEDGE BOOKS

28 Dean Road,

London, N.W.2.